So French!

THE BEST OF FRENCH CUISINE

Sonia Ezgulian

LES CUISINIÈRES

1er Avril
— Les Cigognes en Alsace
CHAMONIX-MONT-BLANC – La Mer de Glace vue de Montenvers

From Brittany's coasts to Savoie Mountains,
from the Alsatian meadows to the Basque shores,
through every France country landscape,
cooks always had one common point: the happiness
from preparing generous and delicious recipes,
be they simple or sophisticated, ancient or creative.
This craft has been passed down from generation
to generation through skills and secrets which have
been gathered in this book and that will show you
a world of taste, discoveries and nostalgia.
You will find in this cookbook a range of regional
recipes, from first course to dessert, which reflects
above all one of the most important aspect of good
cooking, that which give the sensibility and
the intuition of a good cook: the desire to share
with the others.

Bon appétit!

Table des Recettes

* **Entrées** First Courses

* **Plats et accompagnements** Main dishes

Entrées
First Courses

La vraie salade niçoise

Anchovies summer salad

Serves 4

- 4 ripe tomatoes
- 4 hard-boiled eggs
- A dozen anchovy fillets in oil
- 1 green pepper
- 3 small green onions

- 1 garlic clove
- A bunch of basil
- A handful of pitted black olives
- A dash of olive oil

Cut each tomato into 6 wedges and salt them lightly. Cut the eggs into quarters and finely mince the green pepper. Chop the green onions and strain the anchovies. Rub 4 soup plates with the garlic clove, which has been cut in half. Place the tomatoes in rose on the plate and salt them lightly again, place the eggs, then anchovy fillets and scatter the olives and the chopped green onions over it.
Prepare the sauce by mixing the olive oil with the chopped basil leaves, salt and pepper. Drizzle the sauce over the salad.
You may add canned tuna to this typical salad from the Côte d'Azur.

Salade de lentilles vertes du Puy

Green lentils salad

Serves 4

- 400 g (14 oz) Puy green lentils
- 1 big onion
- 50 g (1 3/4 oz) ham
- 30 g (1 oz) lard
- 1 bouquet garni* (p. 62)
- 250 g (9 oz) smoked streaky bacon
- 3 shallots
- 1 tablespoon mustard
- 3 tablespoon wine vinegar
- 120 ml (4 fl oz) fruity walnut oil

Put lentils in cold water. Peel and mince the onion, and dice the ham. Brown the ham and onion with fat in a casserole dish. Add the lentils and twice as much water with the bouquet garni. Salt lightly and let simmer. When the lentils are cooked, let them cool for 20 minutes. In the meantime, dice the bacon, brown it in a frying pan and add the chopped shallots. Prepare the vinaigrette dressing with the mustard, the vinegar, pepper and walnut oil. Pour lentils, bacon and shallots in it and adjust the seasoning if needed.

Quiche Lorraine

Egg and bacon pie

Serves 4 to 6

- 300 g (11 oz) piecrust pastry
- 300 g (2 cups) crème fraîche* (p. 62)
- 4 eggs
- 250 g (9 oz) lardons* (p. 62) or lean smoked bacon
- A pinch of nutmeg
- Butter

Place the pastry in a pie plate. Prick it with a fork. Cut the lardons or the smoked bacon into small slabs and stir-fry in the butter. Whip the eggs into an omelet, add the crème fraîche, salt and pepper and the grated nutmeg. Add the lardons and pour this mixture into the plate. Put into the oven at 350 °F for 25 minutes. The quiche must be creamy and lightly browned on the top. Serve very hot.

Pissaladière

Anchovies and olive pie

Serves 4

- 300 g (10 1/2 oz) bread dough
- 10 big onions
- 4 garlic cloves
- A few savory sprigs
- A dozen salted anchovies fillets
- A handful of black olives
- 150 ml (5 fl oz) olive oil

Peel and finely mince the onions. Put them in a frying pan with olive oil, garlic cloves cut in half and savory sprigs. Let the onions simmer at very low heat and stir frequently until they are perfectly stewed. Season with salt and pepper, then remove the garlic cloves and savory sprigs. Stretch the dough to have a 30 cm diameter disk. Put it into the oven for 10 minutes to 400 °F. Cover with the stewed onions and spread the anchovies and the black olives over the tart, then put it back into the oven at 350 °F for 15 minutes.

Serve while it is still warm.

OEufs mimosa

Eggs with mayonnaise

Serves 4

- 8 eggs
- 1 tablespoon white vinegar
- 125 g (4 1/2 oz) tuna
- 100 g (1/2 cup) mayonnaise (p. 61)

Hard-boil the eggs, add and remove the shells.
Cut them in half lengthwise and remove the yolks.
In a plate, crumble the yolks with a fork and mix half of it with mayonnaise.
Add this preparation in the eggs where the yolks were, and top with the remaining yolks crumbled over each egg.

Escargots de Bourgogne en coquille

Garlic buttered snails

Serves 8

- 8 dozens of Burgundy snails
- 500 g (17 3/4 oz) coarse salt
- 500 ml (2 cups) vinegar
- 1 bottle of Burgundy white wine
- 1 onion studded with a clove
- 2 carrots
- 1 bouquet garni* (p. 62)
- 4 garlic cloves

For the garlic butter:

- 750 g (26 1/2 oz) butter
- 80 g (3 oz) parsley
- 40 g (1 1/2 oz) shallots
- 20 g (3/4 oz) garlic
- 20 g (3/4 oz) breadcrumbs

In Burgundy, the live snails are prepared as follows:
Clean the snails (they must not have eaten for the last 24 hours) with running water and remove their cap. Let them disgorge 10 hours in salt and vinegar to get rid of the mucus, then rinse them again and put them 30 minutes in simmering water. Extract

the meat from the shell, remove the black tip and rinse a third time. Put the snails in a casserole dish with three times their height of water. Add the wine, the onion, the carrots, the bouquet garni and the garlic cloves. Season with salt and pepper. Cover and let it cook for 3 hours.
Meanwhile, boil the shells 30 minutes in a large volume of water. Let it cool and remove the impurities.
To prepare the garlic butter, the butter must be at room temperature. Mince parsley, shallots and garlic and mix it with the butter. Add salt and pepper. Mix with the breadcrumbs, then put a curl of butter and a snail in a shell, and fill the shell with the garlic butter. Heat in the oven, in a snail plate, until the butter has melted and start to sizzle.

Flammekiieche

Cream and bacon pie

Brown the onions in butter, mix them with crème fraîche and season lightly. Cut the smoked bacon into lardons* (p. 62) and stir-fry quickly. Spread the dough until it is thin enough, pour the crème fraîche and onions preparation, drizzle with oil and sprinkle with lardons. Place on a large plate and cook into a very hot oven over 400 °F, close to the maximum gas mark, until it starts to brown lightly.

Serves 4 to 6

- 450 g (1 lb) bread dough
- 200 g (1 3/4 cup) crème fraîche* (p. 62)
- 1 tablespoon rapeseed oil
- 2 onions
- A big slice of lard or smoked bacon
- A pinch of grated nutmeg
- Butter

Soupe gratinée à l'oignon

Onion soup with cheese

Serves 4

- 1 beef stock cube
- 4 medium onions
- 15 g (1 tablespoon) butter
- 15 g (2 tablespoons) flour
- 4 slices of sourdough bread
- 70 g (3 1/2 oz) gruyere cheese, grated
- Salt
- Pepper

Plunge the stock cube in a pan of boiling water. Peel the onions and finely slice them. In a large pan, melt butter and add the onions to lightly brown them at low temperature. Dust with flour and cook it a few minutes while stirring. Pour the hot beef broth. Cook it for about 25 minutes.

In the meantime, toast bread slices. Preheat an oven shelf. Put the slices of bread in a large soup tureen, or in 4 small tureens. Pour the soup over it and season with salt and pepper. Spread grated cheese over the soup, and place it in the oven for a few minutes until you get a browned crust on the top.

Beignets de courgettes

Zucchini fritters

Serves 4

- 4 Zucchinis
- 250 g (2 1/2 cups) flour
- 2 eggs
- 200 ml (6 3/4 fl oz) milk
- 1 tablespoon olive oil
- Groundnut oil (for frying)
- 1 packet of baking powder

In an oven dish, pour the flour and make a well. Add a pinch of salt, olive oil, eggs and baking powder in the well. Mix these ingredients and add the milk gradually. Leave the dough to rest. Peel the zucchinis and cut them in slices. Dip the slices in the dough, then in the hot frying oil.

Fry the fritters in oil for 4 to 5 minutes, then drain them on a paper towel.

Salt lightly and serve.

Œufs en meurette

Eggs in wine sauce

Serves 6

- 6 eggs
- 200 g (7 oz) smoked bacon lardons
- 6 bread slices
- 1 garlic clove

- 3 onions
- 5 shallots
- 75 g (3/4 cup) flour
- 750 ml (3 cups) Burgundy red wine

In order to prepare the meurette sauce, slowly stir-fry lardons until they lose their fat with minced garlic cloves, onions and shallots. Sprinkle flour over it and keep stirring. Add salt and pepper and cook at low temperature for 30 minutes.

Meanwhile, boil water with a dash of vinegar and poach the eggs during 4 minutes. Strain the eggs immediately. Grill slices of bread with a bit of garlic rubbed on it and place the eggs over the slices. Cover with meurette sauce and serve.

If you are looking for a drink to accompany the recipe, you may drink the same wine that was used for the sauce.

Plats
et accompagnements
Main dishes

La blanquette de veau

Veal stew

Serves 4 to 6

- 1 kg (2 1/4 lbs) veal breast
- 500 ml (17 fl oz) poultry broth
- 2 carrots
- 2 onions
- 6 button mushrooms
- 2 knobs of butter
- 200 g (1 cup) thick cream
- Lemon juice
- 1 egg yolk
- 1 tablespoon flour
- 1 cup white wine

Cut the meat into cubes and stir-fry with a knob of butter until it starts to brown.
Dust the meat with flour and stir for a while.
Pour white wine and poultry broth, and cook about 20 minutes.
Chop carrots and onions (remove the core) in small dices. Blend them in the pan with the meat and cook a low temperature for about 1 hour. Add finely chopped mushroom, previously sweated in a knob of butter.
Keep on the stove for about 20 minutes.
In a bowl, mix thick cream, egg yolk and lemon juice. Mix this preparation with the meat just before it is served and stir to thicken the sauce.

Potée Auvergnate

Pork stew

Serves 4

- 500 g (17 1/2 oz) slightly salted pork belly
- 1 slightly salted boneless pork shoulder
- 10 peppercorns
- 1 onion
- 2 cloves
- 2 garlic cloves
- 1 bouquet garni* (p. 62)
- 800 g (1 3/4 lbs) carrots
- 800 g (1 3/4 lbs) potatoes
- 3 turnips
- 4 leeks
- 1 small cabbage
- 1 cooked sausage

Put pork belly and pork shoulder in a large stew pot and cover with water. Blanch the meats for 5 minutes, remove the meats from the stew pot and wash it. Put the meats back into the stew pot, cover again with cold water and bring it to the boil. Skim and add pepper, peeled onion studded with cloves, peeled garlic and the bouquet garni. Cover the pot and let it simmer for about 1 hour and a half. Peel carrots, potatoes and turnips. Clean the leeks and tie them into bunches. Remove the cabbage's first leaves, then cut it in quarters and remove the core.

Blanch the cabbages quarters 3 minutes in salted water and drain them and set them aside. When the meats are done, add into the meat broth the cabbage quarters, the leeks, the carrots and the turnips and cook it for 1 hour and a half. Prick the sausage with a fork to prevent it from shattering and add it into the broth 30 minutes before the potatoes are cooked. Season, especially with pepper, as the meats are salty. Serve in a large deep dish.

Hachis parmentier

Mashed potatoes and meat with cheese

Serves 4

- 500 g (17 1/2 oz) meat
- 1 kg (2 1/4 lbs) potatoes
- 1 onion
- 30 g (1 oz) butter
- 30 g (1 oz) grated gruyere cheese
- A bit of parsley

Finely chop the onion and stir-fry it with butter without coloring it. Mince the meat and mix it with the onion and some chopped parsley.
Prepare mashed potatoes.
In an oven dish, place a layer of mashed potatoes, a layer of meat and then another layer of mashed potatoes. Spread grated cheese and small bits of butter on top of your dish and cook for 20 minutes at 350 °F.

Bœuf bourguignon

Beef and wine stew

Serves 6

- 1.5 kg (3 lbs) beef chuck
- 250 g (9 oz) bacon
- 1 bottle of red wine
- 3 carrots
- 150 g (5 oz) pearl onions
- 2 garlic cloves
- 300 g (10 oz) mushrooms
- 1 bouquet garni* (p. 62)
- 15 g (1 tablespoon) butter
- 30 g (2 tablespoons) flour

Remove the salt from the bacon if needed. Chop the beef into cubes and the bacon into lardons. Finely chop the carrots, the onions and the mushrooms. Brown the meat with butter in a casserole dish. Remove the meat and brown the lardons, then the carrots and the onions. Put the meat back into the casserole and dust with the flour, mix thoroughly. Baste with the wine, season and add the peeled and mashed garlic cloves as well as the bouquet garni. Cover and cook for 45 minutes. Sweat the mushrooms in butter and add them in the last 30 minutes. Adjust the heat to give a good consistency to the sauce.

Cassoulet

Beans and meat dish

Serves 6

- 1 kg navy beans
- 600 g (21 oz) Toulouse sausage
- 4 candied duck quarters
- 1 piece fresh pork rind
- 4 carrots
- 500 g (17 1/2 oz) pork belly
- 2 big onions
- 5 shallots
- 1 garlic bulb
- 1 bunch of flat-leaf parsley
- 2 tablespoons duck grease

Drown the navy beans in water during a whole night. The following day, cook them in a large casserole dish for about 30 minutes in salted water with the tied bunch of parsley. It makes the broth tastier. Add the onions, the carrots and the shallots, all diced, and cook for 30 more minutes. In a large frying pan, place the candied duck quarters, add the minced onion, the Toulouse sausage, the chopped garlic and the pork belly. Cook at low heat for 45 minutes. Rub a large oven dish with the duck grease, cover the bottom with pork rind and place half the beans with a bit of their broth. Cover with the meats, and cover again with the remaining beans. Cook in the oven at 350 °F, regularly baste with broth and gravy. Finally, sprinkle chopped parsley over the dish when you take it out of the oven.

Brandade Nîmoise

Salt cod cooked in oven

Serves 8

- 1 kg salt cod
- 200 ml (6 3/4 fl oz cup) olive oil
- 400 ml (2 cups) milk
- 1 garlic clove
- A bit of nutmeg

Remove the salt of the codfish by soaking it in water for a whole night (change the water several times).
Poach the codfish 10 minutes in simmering water.
Strain and "peel" the flesh in an oven dish.
Mash with a spatula, delicately moving the fish while pouring olive oil in a thin trickle, then blend the lukewarm milk the same way. Season with pepper, garlic and nutmeg.
Put the dish in the oven for 5 minutes at 400 °F to brown the brandade.

Fricassée de poulet à l'angevine

Cream chicken

Serves 6

- A chicken, carved into 8 pieces
- 200 ml (1 cup) white vine (ideally from Anjou)
- 60 g (2 oz) butter
- 12 pearl onions
- 250 g (9 oz) small button mushrooms
- 1 lemon
- 15 cl (1/2 cup) crème fraîche* (p. 62)

Brown on each side the chicken pieces in a frying pan at high temperature in a tablespoon of butter. Clean the frying pan and slightly brown the peeled onions. Put back the chicken into the frying pan and spray with wine and season. Cook at low temperature for 30 minutes, flipping the chicken halfway. Sear the mushrooms in a pan with the left over butter. When the poultry is done, remove it again from the frying pan, blend crème fraîche and mushrooms in the pan and reduce. Deglaze with lemon juice. Serve the chicken pieces on a hot dish and cover with the sauce when it is thick enough.

Elsässerin. - Alsacienne.

Choucroute à l'Alsacienne

Fermented cabbage and meat dish

Serves 8

- 2 kg (4 1/2 lbs) raw pickled cabbage
- 2 onions
- 3 tablespoon grease
- 15 juniper berries
- 1 smoked pork belly
- 1 smoked boneless pork shoulder
- 1 Morteau sausage
- 400 g (14 oz) smoked shoulder ham
- 3 cumin seasoned sausages or 6 Montbéliard sausages
- 8 Frankfurt sausages
- 12 medium potatoes
- 2 bottles of riesling (Alsatian wine)

The day before, place the smoked pork belly, pork shoulder and shoulder ham in a large saucepan with cold water for the night.
The next day, rinse the pickled cabbage with cold water, put it in a big volume of boiling water and drain immediately. Chop the onions roughly and cook them at low heat in the grease until they are translucent. Add pickled cabbage and juniper berries. Heat slowly, add 3/4 of the first bottle of Riesling and add pepper to your taste. Mix the three

meats still soaked in the middle of the pickled cabbage, cover the pan and cook at low heat. Be careful of the bottom of the pan, it mustn't stick, add more riesling if needed. After 3 hours, add the Morteau sausage and the pricked sausages to prevent them from shattering while cooking. 20 minutes before the end, add the Frankfurt sausages on the top. In a large warm dish, display the carved meats on the pickled cabbage. Finally, garnish with steamed potatoes.

La vraie ratatouille

Vegetables stew

Serves 6

- 1 kg (2 1/4 lbs) ripe tomatoes
- 6 zucchinis
- 3 eggplants
- 3 peppers
- 4 white onions
- 4 garlic cloves
- A pinch of sugar
- A bunch of parsley
- 1 laurel leaf

Mash the peeled garlic, finely chop the onions, chop the peppers, slice the zucchinis, dice the eggplants and mash the tomatoes with a food mill.
Sweat the onions with olive oil in a frying pan, add the garlic and the pepper, the tomatoes flesh, the laurel and the sugar. Cook at low heat.
In the meantime, stir-fry the eggplants and the zucchinis in a pan with olive oil. Be careful not to mash the vegetables. When the eggplants and zucchinis are done, put them in the frying pan the tomato and pepper sauce. Cook at low temperature for 15 minutes. Serve cold or hot, with minced parsley sprinkled on top.

Bouillabaisse

Fish stew and soup

Serves 8

- For the soup
- 2 kg (5 lbs) small fish (wrasses, small scorpion fish, conger eels)
- 250 ml (1 cup) olive oil
- 2 celery strands
- 2 tomatoes
- 1 garlic bulb
- 1 leek
- 2 onions
- 1 bouquet garni* (p. 62)
- 1 small chili
- A pinch of saffron

For the garnish

- 4 kg (9 lbs) scorpion fish, John Dory fish, weever, gurnard or monkfish
- 1 kg (2 1/4 lbs) potatoes
- Some bread (preferably a French baguette)

For the rouille sauce

- 4 egg yolks
- 6 garlic cloves
- 1 small chili
- A pinch of saffron
- 250 ml (1 cup) olive oil

Peel and chop the vegetables for the soup. Clean out, scale and rinse the fish for the soup. In a large casserole dish, sweat the chopped vegetables in olive oil. Add the fish, season and cook for 10 minutes at high temperature, stirring with a wooden spoon until you get a dough-like consistency. Add the bouquet garni, the chili and 3 liters of boiling water. Stir

and simmer for 40 minutes. Pour the soup through a strainer, pressing the vegetable and the fish with your ladle to extract all their juice, simmer the broth while adding the saffron. Peel and cut the potatoes in thick slices and cook them at low heat for 30 minutes in a bit of saffron seasoned broth.
Make the rouille sauce by mashing the garlic in a mortar with the chili and the saffron. Season and add the egg yolks, then whip them and add gradually the olive oil until the mix thickens. Poach the fish (scorpion fish, gurnard, etc.) cut in pieces for 10 minutes in a bit of saffron broth. Slice the bread, and rub them with garlic then toast them. Serve hot in a large dish, with the potatoes, the rouille sauce and the bread in separate dishes.

Fondue savoyarde

Bread dipped in melted cheese mix

Serves 4 to 6

- 450 g (1 lb) Comté cheese
- 450 g (1 lb) Beaufort cheese
- 450 g (1 lb) Emmental cheese
- Pieces of stale bread
- 1 garlic clove
- 1 dry white vine bottle
- 120 ml (1/2 cup) brandy
- A bit of grated nutmeg

Cut all the cheeses in strips and blend them together. Rub the fondue pan with garlic and pour 3/4 of the wine bottle in it. Heat at low temperature.
When the wine starts to foam, keep stirring with a wooden spatula while you add the cheeses. Season with pepper. When all the cheese has melt and becomes smooth and consistent, add the brandy and the grated nutmeg.
Serve on a stove or ideally in a fondue pan.
To eat the fondue, prick a piece of bread and put it into the pan to cover it with cheese.
When there is no more bread but there is still cheese, you can cook an egg in the pan, mix it with the cheese and eat the mix with a spoon.

Gratin de macaronis à la lyonnaise

French mac & cheese

Serves 4

- 300 g (11 oz) macaroni pasta
- 15 g (1 tablespoon) butter
- 100 g (3 1/2 oz) grated gruyere cheese
- 500 ml (2 cups) whole milk
- 250 ml (1 cup) liquid crème fraîche* (p. 62)
- 12 g (1 tablespoon) flour

Cook the pasta in a large volume of salted water for 8 to 10 minutes, strain them and cool them with trickling cold water.
Mix milk and crème fraîche, start to heat the preparation. Melt butter in a saucepan, add flour. Keep stirring and pour the milk and crème mix when it is hot. Season with salt and pepper. Add the pasta while you keep stirring.
Pour the pasta coated with sauce in an oven dish, trickle with grated gruyere all over the dish and cook in the oven for approximately 10 minutes, until the gratin has a light brown color on the top.

Gratin dauphinois

Potatoes with cream

Serves 4

- 1.6 kg (3 1/4 lbs) potatoes
- 1 garlic clove
- 15 g (1 tablespoon) butter
- 200 ml (1 cup) milk
- 400 ml (2 cups) crème fraîche* (p. 62)
- Nutmeg
- Salt and pepper

Preheat the oven to 350 °F. Peel the potatoes and cut them into thin slices. Peel the garlic clove and cut it in half. Grip an oven dish with the garlic and spread butter. In a bowl, mix the milk and the crème fraîche. Distribute the potato slices in the oven dish so that they cover the bottom and overlap each other. Season with salt, pepper and grated nutmeg. Pour the milk and crème mix over the potatoes. Cook in the oven for 1 hour and 30 minutes. Serve hot.

Grand aioli

Salt cod and vegetables with garlic sauce

Serves 6

- 1 large salt cod fillet
- 3 dozens of cooked whelks
- Some cooked octopus and squids
- Some carrots
- Runner beans
- Zucchinis
- Small artichokes
- Potatoes
- Cherry tomatoes
- As many hard-boiled eggs as you want
- Large sourdough bread slices

For the aioli sauce:

- 12 garlic cloves
- 2 egg yolks
- 200 ml (1 cup) olive oil
- 1 lemon

Soak the cod the day before to leach out the salt (change the water several times).
Poach the fish for 10 minutes just before adding the aioli in order to serve it lukewarm.
To prepare the aioli sauce, peel the garlic cloves, remove the eyes, finely chop them and mash them in a mortar with a pinch of salt. When the mix has a texture similar to an ointment, pour it in a salad bowl, blend the egg yolks in and add 100 ml of olive oil gradually while whipping the sauce to give it a thicker texture. Add the lemon juice.
Steam all the vegetables and put them in a separate dish and the fish in another dish. Serve with hard-boiled eggs and slices of sourdough bread.

Desserts
MADELEINES de COMMERCY

Madeleines de Commercy

Small butter cakes

Serves 4

- 150 g (1 cup 1/2) flour
- 150 g (5 1/4 oz) butter
- 150 g (5 1/4 oz) sugar
- 4 eggs
- An orange peel or a teaspoon of orange flower water

Soften the butter until it has a creamy texture with a spatula. Blend the sugar in and cream together. Add the eggs one by one and mix until combined. Add the flour with the orange peel or the orange flower water. Let the pastry rest for 1 hour at room temperature. Pour the pastry in buttered and floured madeleine molds. Fill the pans two thirds. Bake in the oven at 350 °F for 10 minutes. The pastry will inflate and a small bump will appear on the top of each cake. Remove from the pans and let cool down on a baking tray. Serve plain or with ice cream or with fromage blanc.

Kouign-amann

Butter cake

Serves 8

- 500 g (5 cups) wheat flour
- 15 g (1 tablespoon) baker's yeast
- 400 g (14 oz) butter
- 100 ml (1/2 cup) lukewarm water
- 350 g (1 cup 1/2) sugar
- Salt

Pour the flour in a large mixing bowl with a pinch of salt. Make a well in the middle of the flour. Dilute the yeast with water and add it in the well. Knead for 5 minutes, make a ball with the pastry and let it rest 30 minutes. Dust your kitchen counter lightly and flatten the pastry ball on it with your hands. Put the softened butter in the middle and spread it to have one regular layer of butter on your pastry. Add 200 g sugar over it. Fold the edges of the pastry over this butter and sugar layer. Shape with your palms to get a stretched rectangle, fold it 3 times and cover with a clean towel. Let it rest 15 minutes. Flatten the pastry and fold it 3 times once again, then let it rest 15 minutes. Repeat this step one more time. Grease a pie plate with butter, lightly dust flour over it and place the pastry in the plate. Spread with your hands to cover the whole plate. Drizzle what is left of sugar (150 g) on top of the pastry. Cook in oven for 30 minutes at 400 °F. Serve when the kouign-aman has cooled down a bit.

Les fameuses crèmes brûlées

Burnt cream

Serves 8

- 1 Lt (1/2 pint) milk
- 6 eggs
- 50 g (1 3/4 oz) cornstarch
- 100 g (3 1/2 oz) sugar
- A few orange peels
- A few lemon peels
- A small cinnamon stick
- A star anise
- Brown sugar

Heat the milk with orange and lemon peels, the cinnamon stick and the star anise. When it starts simmering, quickly remove from the heat, cover and let infuse all night.

In a saucepan, whip 2 whole eggs and 4 egg yolks with cornstarch and sugar. Filter the milk with a strainer and pour it on the eggs while you keep stirring. The mixture must be perfectly smooth. Cook it at very low heat and stir with a spatula (do not use a whisk, it will create bubbles). Boil for 2 more minutes and pour the cream in small individual ramekins. Let cool down. Before you serve, dust with brown sugar and caramelize the top of the cream with a hot iron or with a small blowtorch.

Chouquettes maison

Choux buns with pearl sugar

Serves 6

- 150 g (1 cup 1/2) flour
- 150 g (5 1/2 oz) lightly salted butter
- 150 ml (5 fl oz) water
- 150 ml (5 fl oz) milk
- 30 g (2 tablespoon) sugar
- 5 eggs
- 30 g (1 oz) pearl sugar

In a large saucepan, pour milk, water, sugar and diced butter. Bring to the boil at medium heat and pour the flour through a strain and keep stirring with a wooden spoon. Keep stirring for a while. Remove from the stove, add an egg and stir until the pastry becomes homogenous. Repeat for each other egg one after the other.

Place the choux in a pastry bag. On a non-stick pastry plate, place small pastry buns (leave some space between them: the buns will get twice as large when baked). Spread pearl sugar over the buns and place them in the oven at 400 F for 20 minutes. Let them cool down before you serve.

Les bugnes lyonnaises

Sweet fried dough

Serves 8

- 250 g (2 cups 1/2) flour
- 50 g (2 oz) sugar
- 50 g (2 oz) butter
- A pinch of pure salt
- 1 lemon
- 3 eggs
- Groundnut oil
- Icing sugar

Mix the softened butter, the sugar, the salt, the lemon peels and the eggs in a bowl. Dust with the flour while stirring vigorously until you have consistent and smooth dough. If the dough is too hard, add some milk to soften it. Roll it into a ball and let it to rest at cool temperature for 1 hour. Spread the dough and cut rectangles as large as a pack of butter. Make an incision in the middle of each rectangle. Fry them in hot groundnut oil. Remove them, wait for the oil to be hot again and then drown them one more time to have nice crunchy bugnes. When they have cooled down, dust with icing sugar and serve.

LYON. — *Le Palais de Justice et le Côteau de Fourvière.*

La tarte fine aux pommes

Apple pie

Serves 4 to 6

- 4 apples
- 50 g (1 3/4 oz) butter
- 150 g (3/4 cup) brown sugar
- 200 g (7 oz) puff pastry

Spread the pastry and cut four 15 cm discs, and prick them with a fork all over. Place greaseproof paper on the baking tray. Dust with brown sugar under and over the pastry discs. Peel the apples and cut them into thin slices. Place them on the pastry in circle, dust with sugar and spread small butter dices over the pie. Bake in the oven for 15 minutes at 350 °F.

Canelés bordelais

Small caramelized cake

For 15 canelés
- A vanilla clove
- 500 ml (2 cups) milk
- 2 whole eggs
- 2 egg yolks
- 250 g (9 oz) sugar
- 100 g (1 cup) flour
- 50 g (1 3/4 oz) butter + 25 g (3/4 oz) to butter the pans
- 15 ml (1 tablespoon) orange flower water or rum

It is better to use copper molds for this recipe, as the sugar will caramelize all around the cake while it remains soft inside.

The day before, notch the vanilla clove and remove the grains. Bring the milk to boil with the vanilla clove in it. Remove from the stove and let infuse until the next day.

The next day, whip the whole eggs with the egg yolks and the sugar, then dilute with melted butter and orange flower water or rum. Blend the flour in and dilute with the vanilla milk. Pour in the buttered canelés molds and bake for 45 minutes at 350 °F until the cakes starts to Brown. Remove the cakes from their molds and let them cool down.

La tarte aux citrons de Menton

Lemon pie

Serves 6

- 3 Menton lemons
- 200 g (7 oz) sugar
- 4 eggs
- 12 g (1 tablespoon) flour
- Sweet shortcrust pastry

Roll out the pastry in a pie plate. Prick the pastry with a fork, cover it with chickpeas in order to keep the pastry flat and cook it in the oven for 20 minutes at 350 °F. Whip the egg yolks in a mixing bowl with 150 g of sugar until the mix is foaming. Add lemon peels and flour. Boil water in a saucepan and place the bowl on it, cook the cream in it for 15 minutes while stirring. Pour the cream on the pastry. Whip up the egg whites and while you gradually blend in the 50 g of sugar left. Cover the lemon pie with this meringue and cook in a very hot oven for a few minutes until the egg whites are slightly colored. Serve the pie when it has cooled down.

La brioche vendéenne

Butter bread

Serves 6 to 8

- 1 kg (10 cups) flour
- 3 eggs
- 250 g (9 oz) sugar
- 150 g (5 1/4 oz) butter
- 10 g (2 teaspoons) salt
- 36 g (3 tablespoons) crème fraîche* (p. 62)
- 200 ml (1 cup) water
- 40 g (1 1/4 oz) baker's yeast
- 875 ml (3 1/2 cup) milk
- 15 ml (1 tablespoon) orange flower water
- An egg yolk diluted in a bit of milk (to coat)

In a bowl, mix the yeast with the lukewarm milk.
In a salad bowl, mix the flour with sugar, melted butter, add the eggs one after the others, then the milk and the yeast as you keep stirring. Blend the crème fraîche and the orange flower water in and wet with a bit of water so that the pastry is not sticky.
Make a pastry ball and let it rest for 3 hours in a dish covered with a clean kitchen towel at room temperature.
Split the pastry into 2 or 3 parts and put them on a greased baking tray. It can also be baked in a cake mold. Cover the brioche with the egg mixed with

milk using a paintbrush, and put the brioche in the oven for 30 minutes at 350 °F. Make some notches in the brioche and put it back in the oven for 15 more minutes.

Le pain perdu brioché

Butter bread pudding

Serves 4

- 4 thick slices of stale brioche
- 1 egg
- A pinch of cinnamon
- 150 ml (5 fl oz) milk
- 15 g (1 tablespoon) butter
- 15 g (1 tablespoon) brown sugar

Whip the egg with the milk and the cinnamon. Soak the bread slices in this preparation and brown it in a frying pan with the butter and the sugar at the bottom of the pan.

RECETTES DE FRIANDISES
Tôt-Fait
Délayez votre farine avec jaunes d'œufs et lait, puis blancs d'œufs, sucre en
udre, fleur d'oranger, vanille ; faites-en une bouillie épaisse ; versez dans une
urtière largement beurrée et couvrez avec le four de campagne. La pâte monte
mme une omelette soufflée quand elle a été bien préparée.
Les bases
Basics French cuisine

Pâte brisée

Piecrust pastry

- 250 (2 cups 1/2) flour
- 125 g (4 1/2 oz) butter
- 15 ml (1 tablespoon) oil
- 30 ml (2 tablespoons) freezing water
- A pinch of salt
- 50 g (1/4 cup) sugar if you want as sweet pastry

Pour the flour in a bowl and make a well in the middle of it. Add oil, salt and butter chopped in bits in the well. Knead it all with your fingers, adding water sometime to hold the pastry in one part. Shape it into a ball with your hands (go easy, it should not become elastic). Wrap the pastry in plastic wrap and let it rest at least 30 minutes at cool temperature. Butter the pie dish and dust flour over it, then spread your pastry all over the dish.

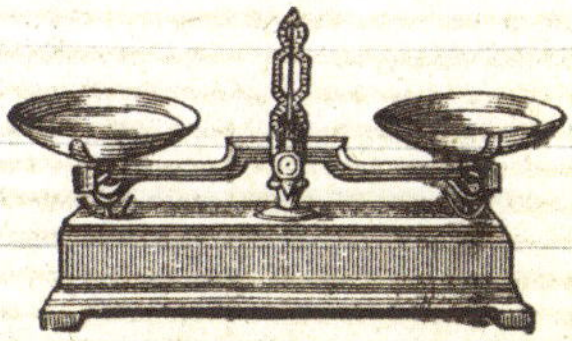

Pâte feuilletée

Puff pastry

- 250 g (2 cups 1/2) flour
- 125 g (4 1/2 oz) water
- 185 g (6 1/2 oz) butter
- A pinch of salt

Pour the flour in a bowl and make a well in the middle of it. Add water and salt in the well. Knead it all with your fingers until you get a homogenous pastry ball. Flatten the pastry into a cross shape. Add the softened butter in the middle. Fold the outer parts of the pastry over the middle. Hit the pastry with a rolling pin to spread the butter evenly. Knead the pastry into a ball, let it rest at cool temperature for 30 minutes.

Spread the pastry lengthwise to give it a vaguely rectangular shape and fold in the extremities to make a square. Let it rest for 30 more minutes at cool temperature.

Rotate the pastry of 1/4 circle, and spread it again lengthwise. Fold the extremities once again.

(Always rotate the pastry in the same direction to get more regular layers).

Pâte sablée

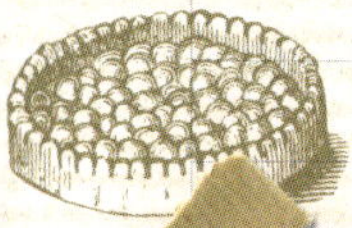

Shortcrust pastry

- 250 g (2 cups 1/2) flour
- 125 g butter (4 1/2 oz) + 20 g (3/4 oz) for the plate
- 70 g (3 oz) sugar
- 1 egg yolk
- Some milk or water
- A pinch of salt

Pour the flour in a bowl and make a well in the middle of it. Add the egg yolk, the salt the sugar and the softened butter in the well. Knead it all with your fingers, adding water or milk progressively to hold the pastry in one part. Shape the pastry into a ball and wrap it in plastic wrap to let it rest 30 minutes at cool temperature. Spread out the pastry with a rolling pin, fold it 2 or 3 times and spread it again to make the pastry suppler. Butter the mold (you may also lightly dust flour over it) and spread the pastry in the mold. Prick it with a fork and bake it 20 minutes in an oven preheated at 400 °F.

This pastry is more convenient for juicy fruits or liquid cream than a pâte brisée.

It can be baked 10 minutes, filled with fruits and baked 10 more minutes. Be careful, when you remove it from its mold, this pastry is very crumbly.

Pâte à pain

Bread dough

- 500 g (18 oz) flour
- 20 g (2 tablespoons) baker's yeast
- 1 teaspoon salt
- 250 ml (8 1/2 fl oz) water

Dilute baker's yeast in lukewarm water. Let it rest 15 minutes. Mix flour and salt, dig a well in the middle of the flour. Pour progressively the yeast and water mix while kneading with the hands until the dough becomes smooth. Shape the dough into a ball, cover it with a towel and let it rest 2 hours at room temperature. Knead again the dough, give it the shape you want and let it rest 2 more hours. Bake for 45 minutes in a preheated oven at 400 °F.

Mayonnaise

- 1 egg yolk
- 1 teaspoon mustard
- Groundnut oil
- Salt
- Pepper

In a bowl, put the egg yolk at room temperature and the mustard. Season with salt and pepper. Start by adding groundnut oil one drop at a time while whipping to emulsify the mayonnaise, then pour a trickle of oil when the mayonnaise has the right consistency.

Bouquet garni

It is a bundle of aromatic plants, often used to add flavour to dishes. The three essential herbs of a bouquet garni are bay leaves, thyme sprigs, but other herbs can be added such as parsley, sage or even celery.
If you can't find bouquets garnis in store, you can make your own by buying the need plants and tying them up with a string!

Lardons

Lardons are tiny rectangular slabs of bacon.
Their shape and size make them easy to add in a dish and they are common in French recipes.
If you can't find lardons in store, just cut them yourself in a pièce of raw bacon.

Crème fraîche

This dairy is very often used in French cuisine.
It is not sterilized, and it must have at least 30% of fat (usually around 40%). Plain yogurt or plain sour cream can be used to replace it in most of the cases, but be aware that the taste will be a little different, so don't hesitate to adjust it to your taste (especially with the sour cream).